Seil Stories

Written by Michael Shaw

Scottish Slate Islands Heritage Trust

SC 029805

Published in 2022 by Scottish Slate Islands Heritage Trust
13a Ellenabeich, Easdale, Oban, PA34 4RQ

www.slateislands.org.uk

Design: Trevor Davies
Artwork: Mike Lowe; www.mike-lowe.co.uk/
Photographs: Page 40, The Mackenzie Collection
All others, Trevor Davies

Cover photo: The view from above the raised beach on the south-west coast of Seil Island to Ellenabeich, with Insh Island beyond and, in the distance, the island of Mull.

PREFACE

Please read this little book as an affectionate, if somewhat oblique, look at Seil Island. The stories were inspired and created by the history, the people, and the spirit of a very special place that has been the author's home for over seventy years. They are supported by Mike Lowe's unique illustrations. The beautiful photographs by Trevor Davies enliven and support the short passages on history and landscape; they seek to give the stories their context.

This little work is offered as an entertainment, but in the hope that the reader leaves with a feeling for the unique spirit of place that Seil derives from the wave after wave of catastrophic change that has swept over the island and its people over two or three millennia. Perhaps that hypnotic spirit is so elusive that only an oblique view can do it justice. Only in retrospect can change be evaluated and understood.

Looking at the history of Seil, it's just not enough to ask what happened?, or why? We're driven to ask - "What was it like for the Seil Islanders of the time? And how does it impinge on us now"?

About thirty years ago, I was asked to be leader of the Kilbrandon Cub Scouts. Told I was the last resort, and that every boy of eligible age in Easdale School was a Cub, it was impossible to refuse. I wasn't a great leader, nor was I very enthusiastic at the time, but memories do grow fonder as the years go by. I mention this only because it was for those Cub Scouts that the original stories were told. Dare I hope they may now be read by their descendants?

Are the stories true? The boys used to ask me that, too. I answer now as I did then: what do you think?

The dike at Puilladobhrain on the north-west coast of Seil.

CONTENTS

Seil Island
(Saoil)
Puilladobhrain
Clachan Sound
Clachan Brid
B844
Ardfad
Ardencaple
Clachan-Seil
Insh Island
Sound of Insh
Surgery
B844
Ellenabeich
Easdale Island
Easdale
Balvicar
Kilbride
Chapel (14th C)
Seil Sound
Ardmaddy Castle
Kilbrandon
Dùn Mucaig
B8003
Portmor
Ballachuan
Firth of Lorne
Cuan
Caisteal nan Con
Torsa
Belnahua
Cullipool
Dùn Fadaidh
Degnish
Fladda
Ballycastle
Loch Melf
Luing
(Luinn)
1 mile

INTRODUCTION

About eight miles south of Oban (as the seagull flies), a fine stone bridge connects the Scottish Mainland to Seil Island. By this bridge, Scotland is also firmly secured to a wonderful string of islands; rather as the clasp might secure a precious pendant to a lady's neck. Those island gems are Seil, Luing, Scarba, Jura and Islay, and they protect the sheltered sea-route for vessels sailing northwards from the Irish Sea and beyond.

Completed in 1792 by John Stevenson of Oban, this "fixed link" is a great convenience for Seil, but also for Luing and Easdale Islands, each of which can be accessed by its own small ferry from Seil. The bridge is itself an attraction for visitors, that for many years, have come to admire its fine high arch, and cross it to enjoy the outstanding landscapes of Seil, gaze upon the views or wonder at the fading legacy of the great slate quarries.

Looking at Seil now, the island's most formative features would seem to have been the Bridge and the Slate Quarries. The one revolutionised travel and the other dramatically changed the landscape, introducing an industrial and quasi-urban society. They remain the iconic images of Seil. But in the long view, neither bridge nor quarries appear to be the primary makers of Seil's special character and spirit.

Even without a bridge, there was always, at low tide, a crossing place for livestock, horses, and folk on foot. A wheeled vehicle couldn't cross without a bridge, but until the 18th century, there were few roads fit for wheeled traffic anyway. The short and shallow crossing, wet and cold as wading across might be, was a natural "fixed link", doing the same job as the man-made version today. Long-distance travel and the carriage of goods were always much better achieved by sea, even a hundred years after the bridge was built.

Slate ultimately did play a dramatic part in our story. Initially only supplemental to farming and fishing, it was by the late 18th century, hugely destructive of the landscape, and brought vast social change. Slate income built the villages, the roads, and the famous bridge. Hundreds of men and families came to labour in the quarries and swell the island population. Barely two hundred years later, the last quarry closed; but today, with evidence of the destruction fast disappearing, some of the social infrastructure remains.

For the motor car age the bridge is vital, but for much longer it was the natural "fixed link" that uniquely exploited Seil's prime position on the sheltered sea-route. That gave our island a special advantage over all the others, and therefore most defined its history and spirit. Seil was a unique conduit for all the news, gossip and momentous events that were played out on Scotland's Western Seaboard. People always came to Seil.

The earliest arrivals settled after the Ice-Ages and clashed with subsequent incomers, with whom they often made peace and even married. Picts, Britons and Gaels, Vikings and Anglo-Normans, fought their battles here, part of the violent struggle for the Scottish Crown. Throughout these turbulent centuries more incomers were washed, like debris from a storm at sea, to settle on the shores of Seil. Only after the 1745 Jacobite uprising did government finally tame the Highland warlords; establishing a rule of law that had been normal in the South for a century before. The population rose as quarrying grew, only to dwindle as production failed. Seil was always a place of coming and going. New sights, new ways, new people.

Look again; observe how the landscapes tells us tales of forts, furrows, and great works, and speaks of warriors, quarriers and farmers, down the ages.

The Bridge Over the Atlantic giving access from the mainland (left) to to the east coast of Seil Island (right).

m.P. Lowe

THE GOOD NEWS

Maelchon stared moodily across Seil Sound. Sitting sheltered from the wind, near the narrow and half hidden bay that served as private haven for his people, he could look across Port Mòr and watch little white horses being kicked up by a brisk westerly. The fort of Dun Fadaidh, perched high up above the far side of the Sound, was never far from his thoughts, and always there to mock him, even in his private haven.

Maelchon had two children, his son, Nectan, and his daughter Thana. They were twins, whose mother had died at their birth. It was his life's ambition to build for them a great inheritance and a great prestige. He had already come far, moving West from Caledonia in the service of a Pictish warlord, and being a good and ruthless servant, was rewarded with a little domain near Ballachuan Loch, just inland from the haven in Port Mòr. Protected by his powerful benefactor, he had prospered in that loch-side spot. The land was fertile, and the fishing abundant, attracting new arrivals to swell his little band. Now he wanted more. Seeing the rising power of such forts as Dun Fadaidh, right there, and Ardfad, at the North end of Seil, he asked himself how he could achieve a fort of his own? He would seek out and consult The Wise One, half priest, half scholar, who read the markings of the monoliths, understood the power of charms, and always had the latest news and rumour.

The wise one listened carefully to Maelchon's tale, looking thoughtful and grim: his advice was disturbing.

"Your Pictish sponsor is old news. The Pictish influence of Caledonia is declining, while the sea-borne Gaels come ever more to the fore. They build forts or make treaties with those who have forts and replace the sitting tenants by murder or by marriage. To grow your power, you must learn from these new and powerful neighbours, and make your place among them. I can help and guide you in all this, but it will be hard, and it will be very costly. Give me three days for thought".

After three days, the Wise One revealed his plan. If Maelchon would promise to pay, after ten years, whatever he were asked, the fates would intervene and grant even his wildest wishes. It was a dangerous offer. The Wise One could be relied on to deliver; but the price would be very high and remain undisclosed until the day of reckoning - ten years hence.

Maelchon returned to the loch-side. His beloved children, the twins, were playing at the water's edge. He realised that, as things stood, he could never provide a fitting inheritance for his son Nectan, nor see his lovely daughter Thana, make the grand marriage she deserved. Full of fear, he had no choice. He must accept the offer no matter at what cost. The day of payment was a long way off, like very distant thunder.

Ten years passed: momentous, historic, and sometimes violent. Maelchon dwelt no longer by the loch but, ambitions fulfilled, he now dwelt and ruled at Ardfad, near the North Point of Seil. That fort would one day become an important castle, and even in those far-off times, gave him prestige far beyond the limits of Seil Island. He was a hard, successful, cruel man. The twins' deceased mother had been replaced by a high-born bride from across the Irish Sea, and he now had three additional sons, with their mother's Irish blood. This connection to the Gaelic interest had been key to his advance: a marriage brokered with the Wise One's help. Just sometimes, he missed the simple life they had enjoyed between the loch and the sea, but he'd done it all for his beautiful older children, the twins.

Now, the fateful hour had come. He had received a summons from the Wise One to go once more to the loch-side, and to take the twins with him. The price was to be disclosed: and paid.

Maelchon still strong and upright, set out with Nectan, outwardly like his father but a little gentler and finer of feature, and Thana, tall, elegant, and beautiful. It was a fair walk, almost the full length of Seil Island.

On the way, they came upon a woman: the victim of a fall or perhaps an assault. She was gravely injured, and lay a little off the path, making cries just loud enough to be heard by the two young people. A woman in that world was considered of little importance unless she be of the highest birth, but this was a poor, helpless, hapless creature, of the lowest labouring class, and a dweller in some tiny hovel. Thana turned aside, followed by her brother, but at first their father remained aloofly on the path, following the twins only after some delay. When he arrived crossly at the scene, Thana said no word, but she caught his eye, and for some reason, he relented. Pressed for time as they were, those three fine figures stooped to wrap the woman in one of their costly cloaks and carry her between them. They had a considerable distance to bear their burden before they found a place of safety and some people with whom to leave her.

They arrived beside the loch well after the appointed hour, and as they approached the Wise One's hut, were greeted by the words: "You're late: no matter, it was not time wasted, but we must get to business. Can you guess why I asked you to bring me your noble and beloved twins, my Lord?" Maelchon paled but gave no reply.

"The greatest of all powers" continued the Wise One, "approve of your success, but not of your cruelty. They will take from you nothing you have accrued since they made the deal with you. Their price is simple: the two most precious jewels of all your previous wealth. You will hand over your children, the young Lord Nectan and the lovely Thana".

Before these terrible words had entered Maelchon's devastated understanding, the Wise One continued.

"You have been a hard, cruel man, but in recognition of that one kindness you and your children displayed, upon your journey here, the price will be discounted, and their fate made more glorious. When your twins hear the Good News, they will return to this spot, and later, when their time is come, they will not die, but live on here, a token of the Good News that will redeem mankind for ever."

Maelchon's head swam. To lose his children, to lose that very son for whom he had done all that he had done - for a moment he swooned. When he came to, the twins had gone and there, in the loch, swam two lovely white swans: his precious children.

Maelchon pressed the Wise One for an explanation of the Good News, but alas the Wise One knew not how to help him. From far and wide Maelchon summoned other scholars, and travelled ceaselessly up and down the coast. He distributed wealth to the poor, built shrines, employed healers and mounted expeditions. Time and time again he visited the loch and would be seen speaking to the swans. All to no avail. Gradually he grew old and sick. He lost the confidence of his people and died a broken man. The swans swam on, as young and beautiful as ever.

Six generations passed. People had come and gone, new chiefs had risen and fallen. The old settlement remained little changed, lying quietly between the sea and the loch, now home to a peaceful, modest population.

One summer evening a tiny, fragile boat came up the sound from far away to the South and made a gentle landfall on the shingle of the bay.

M.P. Lowe

Two white swans glided curiously round as the weary traveller came ashore. A couple of women had been collecting mussels and were chatting on the rocks, enjoying the evening sun.

The traveller touched the stones at the women's feet, opened wide his arms and cried "I come to you in the name of Jesus Christ: blessed is he that cometh in the name of the Lord!" and here he crossed himself. The women were a trifle alarmed, and their eyes widened. They had no idea what this was all about. The two swans paddled hard and made little squeals of excitement.

That evening the traveller sat by the fire at the look-out above the bay. He had been well received. A lone traveller was no threat and this one was clearly tired and hungry. His accent was a little strange and unfamiliar, but they understood that he had crossed the sea from Ireland to Kintyre before following the sheltered route north. Importantly, once revived with a stimulating drink and restored by a hearty meal, he began to talk. A little crowd had assembled to hear a visitor that could sing for his supper.

A charismatic narrator, he amazed and entertained them, weaving wisdom and mystery into the visions and characters he described. It was all new and exciting, but strangely compelling and familiar to his captivated listeners.

Describing the shepherds' consternation before the Angelic Choir of the first Christmas, the traveller quoted thus: "Fear not, Good News of great joy I bring…" when suddenly he stopped. Two new figures stood silently above him. They were tall and straight, old certainly, but curiously beautiful and fair.

"Holy man, I am Nectan" announced the taller one. "My sister, Thana, and I, will learn all that you have to teach, and we will dwell here with you as long as we are spared, to help you spread this Good News to all that will receive it".

And so, it transpired. For many years they stayed there and preached the word. Ultimately, they passed away, and the two swans returned to swim upon the waters of Ballachuan Loch. Later a chapel was built nearby, replaced today by Kilbrandon Church, with its glorious stained-glass windows. The swans still rarely desert their watery patrol, and the Good News lives on.

ST NEMO AND THE WHITE MARTYRS

Seil Island lies in the parish of Kilbrandon. The prefix "Kil" denotes a cell or chapel, while "brandon" is for St. Brendan the Navigator, the celebrated Celtic saint who dwelt for a time on Seil. Abundant other examples of such place names suggest that Christianity came here quite early.

The Celtic Church recognised as "White Martyrs" those who left Ireland on dangerous sea-voyages, carrying the Gospel to distant places. St Columba of Iona was one of the most celebrated of such White Martyrs. Saint Brendan, often credited with bringing Christianity to Seil, was another. It seems unlikely that either of these "big guns" was the first to arrive: it's much more likely that the Faith was here before them. "The Good News" is a story in tribute to that earlier, anonymous, "Saint Nemo," who first brought the Good News to Seil.

Today's traveler will want to visit the magnificent stain glass in Kilbrandon Church and afterwards, may look outward from the doorway and see Ballachuan Loch below them, usually with a pair of swans upon the water. Down there, among the rushes to the left of the loch, is a small green mound where the grass, often grazed by sheep, covers the stones of Kilbrandon's oldest church. This is, indeed, believed to be where the great Saint Brendan built his cell, a building too insubstantial to have left ruins.

Beyond the loch, the narrow canal that runs out to the sea was cut through the rock as job creation for the quarry workers during a 19th century recession. It also permits access to the loch by sea trout and contributes to the land drainage all the way back to Balvicar. On the way to the sea, it crosses a green, level area, where a multitude of large stones seem deliberately placed rather than scattered at random. The patterns and lines of stone upon the ground suggest possible activity from the Iron Age through Viking times to the Medieval period and up to the late 19th century, certainly long pre-dating the canal.

These islands were home to a significant population and therefore an attractive opportunity for commerce, plunder, or religious conversion.

The view from Port Mòr looking across Seil Sound to the fort of Dun Fadaidh (just above and slightly right of centre).

M P Lowe

THE CRANNOG

The hillsides and the forests are reflected darkly in the waters of Loch Seil, creating a mirrored and fitting background for the bright water lilies that float upon the surface. Stones, all that remain of the ancient Crannog, protrude from the waters and sparkle in the sunlight, seeming to float upon the inky surface of the loch. Upon those stones stands the cormorant, his wings outstretched like a heraldic crest.

Winter and summer, in rain, or in drought, he is very rarely absent. Indeed, so faithful is he to that spot, and so eternal in his vigil, a fancy has arisen that he is no mortal bird. This is his story: it is he that speaks to us now.

"You see me now as a bird. I am that, of course, but inside, I am something much more. Inside, I am that same young lad, that same, unfortunate boy that ran and swam and laughed and cried, in this same place; nearly twenty centuries ago

This stony perch was very different then. What you see now is but a fragment of the sturdy, man-made island that was home to me and my extended family. We had neighbours of all ages living there as well, and even a little space for livestock when required. Younger, fitter, men would come and go, as work or hunting or more perilous pursuits, permitted. Danger was never far away, but the adults largely ensured that talk of such things was kept from the likes of me.

Warlike raiders were a constant threat to our peaceful and prosperous community. Our livestock, raised in such fertile and sheltered country, could be a temptation to people who eked out just bare existence on higher and harder ground elsewhere. From the coast, not far away, came sea-borne raiders, seeking whatever they might pillage, and ready even to carry off any fit young folk that they could sell or enslave.

I was just twelve years of age, when came the awful day. All the fit men of our family had been called away to join with others and forestall a serious incursion to the South. They would be absent for some days and nights. Only the women, the children and the very old would remain, with only the secret of the loch to keep us safe.

Look again at the waters of the loch. See how they reflect, like a mirror, all that is above, but reveal nothing of what might be lying below. They allow no hint of that vital secret. The causeway to the Crannog was of posts driven into the bed of the loch so that their broad round tops lay out of sight, just below the surface. It was not a straight line but a complicated pattern, twisting and turning all the way. Of course, we knew the route by heart, even as children, and could run swiftly over the invisible pathway raising a fine splash as we did so. But to the stranger, it was a slow and dangerous passage. Even old men and women could pick off any number of attackers, who could approach only very slowly, probing for each step of the secret, serpentine, route.

Before the menfolk departed, they swam the best of the cattle over to the Crannog and left them in our care, chasing the rest so vigorously and so noisily that they scattered and fled up the hill. On departure, the Crannog Headman turned to all who were to stay behind. With particular attention to us children, he warned us urgently that no-one, on pain of severe punishment, must leave the crannog until he came again and gave permission. On shore, we would face the greatest of personal danger; but worse, much worse, a keen eye could watch from the shore and memorise the secret twists and turns of anyone coming or going across the waters.

Alas, at twelve years old I fretted at the very idea of confinement, and very early next morning, I escaped. I made my way very slowly, and without a splash, across the causeway. Once safely on dry land and fearing that one of the old people might have heard me from the crannog, I raced up into the oak forest, and headed at full speed for the coast. Freedom, exercise, and excitement. What a day!

It was high summer, with promise of a warm day, so I headed for the beach at Barnacarry. The children of the landless labourers often played there, so I was sure to find some companions, and, sure enough, I did, in plenty. Together, we spent a long day in the sun; swimming, running, and wrestling on the smooth grey sands until, with a pleasant tiredness setting in, we talked and told stories on the warm rocks.

At dusk I turned homewards, but not at the giddy pace I'd made in the early morning. My footsteps dragged, not just with honest fatigue, but in growing fear of the maternal wrath that would surely await me. My escape without permission would have drawn rebuke at any time, but approaching the summit that overlooks the loch, I recalled, with growing fear, the awful warning given by the departing Headman.

At the Duachy ridge, I stopped; transfixed; a chill hand gripping my very entrails. All fear of parental displeasure evaporated. In the last, grey light of the dying day, the loch lay calm and colourless below me, but no, it was no longer a safe, familiar place. The crannog had gone. My home, which should be there, behind its bark-encrusted palisade, was gone. Blackened stones protruded from the water, in a low, black, and jagged ring. None of the familiar huts remained to offer either punishment or shelter; only thin, twisting, columns of smoke, drifted gently and silently upwards in the darkling, evil-smelling air.

My escape that morning, had gone unseen by my own people, but had been observed from the shore. Attentive and deadly watchers had counted and noted my every footstep. Armed with the secret of our underwater causeway, our foes had rushed and overwhelmed the Crannog. Every occupant had perished or been carried off, and the dwellings torched. My folly had destroyed it all, in one foolish prank.

Holed up in the Duachy scrub. I had no plan, no excuse to make, no story to tell. But even in my despair, a grain of childish confidence remained. When the men returned all would be well. The grown-ups would prevail as grown-ups always do: but it was not to be.

Some time, later our men came back, but by instinct I stayed hidden. When they stopped and saw that devastation, they stood silent for a long while, then they lamented, loudly and bitterly. Finally, turning their backs and walking very slowly, they went away. Seeing their grief, and fearing their rage, I remained in hiding and let them go.

That summer was my last in human form. The cold and wet of early winter fell upon me, hunger gripped me, and fatal sickness quickly followed. No more I play and frolic by the loch. I haunt this place for ever. Bitterly remembering my folly: warmly recalling all that folly has destroyed. Give a thought, reader, to me, a poor restless bird; and to all who perish by folly, greed and war."

M.P. Lowe

Above: Just a few stones show above the surface of Loch Seil to mark the remains of the crannog today.

THE OLD ROAD TO SEIL

The Crannog story is set in a time when the ancient connection between Ireland and Argyll was becoming a factor in the struggle for supremacy between the very different Pictish, British and Irish cultures: a struggle that would curse Scotland for centuries. Those years of political strife provided cover for warlords and rogues to prey on small, poorly defended communities and exploit them for personal profit.

Although most long-distance travellers and all but the lightest of freight must have come and gone from Seil Island by sea; there also appears to have been an important land-route along the West bank of Loch Seil. Following very much the route of our modern road from Oban, the steep hill that climbs up from Kilninver, together with the valley of Loch Seil, form, in effect, a pass between Raera Hill and Duachy Hill, both parts of the high ground running northwards from Loch Melfort and plunging down to the sea between the Toad of Lorne, and Barnacarry. It must always have offered the easiest passage to the coast and the shortest crossing to Seil island.

The importance of that route helps to explain the many ruins and sites nearby. There are ancient standing stones and an early Christian site up on Duachy Hill and, further up near the Toad of Lorne, the ruins of old fortifications. Around Barnacarry, a sandy bay near the entrance to Loch Feochan, there is copious evidence of former habitation, including the remains of the somewhat later quarrying and manufacturing of millstones.

The bare stones in loch Seil, often barely discernable after heavy rain, are material clues, not just of a crannog, but of how natural topography could permit the perils of national politics to impinge so gravely upon simple, peaceful people who lived here long ago.

From above more of the crannog can be seen submerged below the surface.

J.M.P. Lowe

THE FAIRY CAVE

The West coast of Seil, from the opening of Cuan Sound, round to Easdale Island, takes the form of a raised beach lying between the ocean's edge and a steep, rocky escarpment. On that windswept beach, around half a mile North of Cuan, the ancient fort of Dun Mucaig is easily spotted, but its near-vertical and narrow access is not easily ascended. Finding the cave, which is quite close to the fort, can be very difficult indeed. A low fissure in the cliff is the entrance to a mysterious, deep, dark passage. A few feet in, the head room rises enough for an adult to walk upright, but descending into the darkness that headroom decreases and the passage narrows, so that a section of the descent, about half-way down the passage, is a very tight squeeze.

As children, we loved that cave, and would climb over the hill in high hopes of finding it, often without success, so we just had to be content with scaling the heights of Dun Mucaig. With that elusive nature and the mysterious story we had heard; we came to call it "The Fairy Cave".

We had been told that - "Once upon a time, a piper volunteered to go down the cave with his little dog. As man and beast disappeared in the subterranean darkness, the sound of pipes receded slowly and fell silent. Alas, the piper was never seen again, but later the animal re-appeared some eight miles distant, on the Isle Mull, without a hair on its body" .

I heard that little story seventy years ago, and it was very old, even then. Furthermore, it seems to have been well and widely known even in the far-off times when Viking raiders from the sea brought nightmares to the good people of Seil.

At that time there lived around the fort, a large family or tribe of murky reputation and suspicious habits. Their comings and goings were unexplained, and they usually appeared to have money. Most of them were tall, fair, and wiry, and they claimed to have come from "down about Kintyre". Not everyone was convinced by that claim, but they were tolerated mainly as potential deterrent against the Vikings and similar marauders. They certainly kept good watch from the vantage point of Dun Mucaig.

This family, commonly referred to as the Beach-People, were the sole occupants of all that raised beach, save that one rough little hut was home to an aged and rather disabled lady. This lady, usually known as Mistress Waverly, was rumoured to be of high birth and origins, with powerful connections and special powers of healing and wisdom.

During a spell of strong southwest winds, early one winter, when the days were short and wild, most of the male Beach People were away from Dun Mucaig, leaving only a couple of reliable young fellows to keep watch and look after the women and children. One morning these two young men paid a visit to Mistress Waverly, and their story was a grave one.

Elif the Raider with a shipload of his Vikings was heading for Seil. Word must be got to the absent Beach People, who were in Mull. They must come immediately and bring reinforcements. This would require a dangerous return trip to Mull; difficult in that weather, and impossible to complete before the raiders could strike.

The old woman, after a minute's thought, began the familiar tale of the piper and his dog. Seeing the weary look that appeared in the eyes of the young men, she raised her finger:

"Listen well, there is more to that old story than you could ever guess. Right now, it may be the only road to survival for you and all who live on Seil and Easdale".

The entrance to the Fairy Cave.

Rebuked, the boys stood quietly and heard her to the end. Indeed, they learnt much, and it was full of hope that they took their leave.

Within the hour, the Beach People had gathered up their valuables, grabbed some food and skins of water and hurried to the Fairy Cave. Having found the entrance, they walked down the passage 'till they had to crawl and wriggle through the narrow half-way point. From there the cave opened wider once again and they could move on faster.

At last, they reached the end. They had dragged with them a

The fort of Dun Mucaig sits atop its rocky pinacle on the south-west coast of Seil Island.

rough ladder, and this they lifted against the rock. Very high up, in the right-hand corner of what seemed a solid wall, there was a tiny aperture. It was reasonably adequate for the passage of a child, but a real struggle for the adults to get through. Stripping off their outer coats, they made it. The ladder was drawn up and pulled after the fugitives, well into the narrow gap, leaving only the two young men outside. The fugitives inside then thrust a large stone into the gap and packed it with smaller stones. From the outside, no sign of the high-up entrance could be seen and no amount of tapping on solid lower rock could betray the secret of the continuing cave.

The young men hurried up the cave to the distant triangle of light where they wasted no time and soon their fragile little boat was rising bravely to the seas, headed for Mull and for the hope of reinforcements.

As dusk fell that evening a loud clamour arose outside Mistress Waverly's hut. "Come in Elif the Raider," she called out, "A harmless old crone like me has nothing to fear: how can I help you?"

The raiders were, of course, seeking information about the Beach People, and though the old lady would not defy them outright, she could play for time. After much procrastination she hinted that the cave might be their target, but pleading its elusive nature, the failing light, and her old age, suggested leaving it 'till daybreak.

Elif agreed but, even at the onset of full daylight on the following day, it was only with great caution that he took his men towards the cave. He feared a trap. To negotiate the passage, and the narrow mid-point, while taking sensible precautions against an ambush, was a slow job. By the time the raiders were forced to admit they couldn't find any clue, the day was far spent. They emerged into the failing daylight, angry and frustrated. Their leader ordered a careful search of the area around, while he concentrated on the woman whom he believed to have had misled him.

Mistress Waverly trusted that her reputation would protect her from serious injury; for even the fearsome Elif had respect for those mysterious powers, if not for any rumours of her high birth. However, not even that respect could persuade him to swallow a fairy tale of dogs, pipers, and a secret route to Mull. He snorted loudly and went off to order an expansion of the search.

It was but a short and wintry day, and darkness soon overtook them. The raiders were forced to spend a second night ashore. Elif, ever the watchful Viking leader, was unhappy about their exposure to sudden attack on unfamiliar ground. He considered taking shelter in the fort, but was suspicious of the narrow, twisting steps and feared a trap there too. He bade his men bed down behind some large outcrops of slate, and set double guards, well briefed to keep a keen look-out to sea: he felt dangerously exposed.

To concentrate on the seaward side was an error Elif would long remember. Just before dawn, the warriors of the Beach People stoutly reinforced by friends from Mull, landed quietly at a point well North of Dun Mucaig. From the landward side, their attack was sudden and in force. Elif fled to his ship having lost more of his raiders than he could afford. Clear of Seil Island and out of danger, Elif gave deep thought to the failure of his raid. Those reinforcements had indeed come from Mull. Could there be some truth in that old story of the piper, the dog, and the cave?

M.P.Lowe '14

FORT, CAVE AND 400 VIKING YEARS

The fort at Dun Mucaig is a good landmark for locating the Fairy Cave. About halfway along the raised beach between Cuan and Seaview, on the Easdale road. It's a rewarding, undemanding walk, despite there being no footpath. The whole distance is around one and a half miles, and all the way the eye is drawn irresistibly to the magnificent south-westerly views. The Isle of Mull provides the distant backdrop; appearing as a dark and distant landmass across the Firth of Lorne, crowned by the peaks of Ben More and Ben Buie, but dwindling to the south and growing paler, towards the Ross of Mull and the hidden, sainted, Island of Iona.

The fort sits about halfway along the raised beach, perched atop a rocky column, split by nature from the cliff. A steep and defensively narrow path climbs to the ruin, seriously eroded by time. As youngsters, we persuaded Donald, a Garron pony, to climb right up into the fort. One would hesitate to try it now, even without a pony. The Fairy Cave is about a quarter of a mile north of the Fort and very difficult to find. Inside, it's much as described in the story, with a low entrance and narrow midpoint.

The Vikings played a huge part in the story of Seil. From the 6th century, they were frequent and bloody raiders, and by the 8th century were settled and intermarrying on many of the islands, while bringing fear and violence to the others. Ultimately ruling almost all the Hebrides, they even joined the struggle to control the whole of Scotland, finally withdrawing only after the Battle of Largs in 1263. The "Viking Period", possibly more than 400 years for these islands, left clear traces for us to find: local place-names, obvious engineering remains and a major contribution to the local gene pool. In many respects the impact of the Scandinavian invasions was as significant in the Scottish Islands as was the Norman Conquest of England. Certainly, the legacy was probably deeper and more long lasting than the industrial age of slate in Seil and the Slate Islands, which was at most from 1745 to 1960.

The well hidden entrance to the Fairy Cave.It is behind the base of the fencepost at the far end of the remains of the dry stone wall.

M.P.Low

SEIL TO SERINGAPATAM

Hector Campbell was a handsome, well-built, seventeen-year-old, his companion and foster-brother, Mungo Grant, a small and rather weedy, fifteen. Together, they had come a long way from Seil. Orphaned as little children, they had been rescued by a group of young army officers, who found them a home together on Seil Island. These men had promised a much-loved fellow officer, as he died of wounds after a battle in India, that the motherless boys would be cared for. Thus, the two orphans had been settled on Seil, where they passed their childhood.

Now, in the year 1795, docking at Madras, on the East Coast of India, these young men were marched through the sweltering summer heat to a tented camp near Fort Saint George. They had left their humble island home nearly a year before, by begging a passage from Easdale to Port Glasgow in a small and leaky sailing smack.

At Glasgow, with a large group of recruits for the armies of India, they were embarked on a Royal Navy transport. Some nine months of sailing lay ahead; down to the Barbary Coast, round Africa to Zanzibar, and across the Indian Ocean. Always dependant on wind and weather, with landfalls only for water and rations.

Not all the men had completed their voyage. Some died in foreign ports, seeking strange, exotic pleasures, while others simply jumped ship and deserted. Some were carried off by shipboard fevers, and two were lost overboard. Not all ills were posed by fevers, nor injuries by stormy weather. Such ships of that time would often carry some cruel and desperate men, willing to obtain by violence any little treasure or favour from a shipmate. Hector was once the target of just such an attack, but Mungo forestalled it. Despite his youth, and heeding no threat to his own life, he saw only Hector's mortal danger. Seizing a sharp, splintered belaying pin, he drove it into the assailant's neck. Blood spurted from the wound and the villain came close to death. Fortunately for Mungo, a young surgeon's mate had witnessed the whole encounter. He bound up the wound and reported it officially as an accident. Without that swift intervention, the rogue would certainly have perished, and Mungo most probably have hanged for murder. Hector, unhurt, said little, but he remembered an old Highland saying: "A kinsman is part of a man's body, but a foster-brother is a piece of his heart."

Eleven years earlier, Hector, aged six, and Mungo, aged 4, together with a sixteen-year-old girl to mind them, arrived on Seil Island orphaned, frightened and unloved. Their new home was a smallholding on Ballachuan Township. The occupier, Ewen MacLean, was as poor and as hard as the hovel in which he lived and the stony ground from which he struggled to wring a living. When a young officer of his former regiment had turned up with a proposal that might relieve his poverty, he had no choice but to accept. He had agreed, in exchange for a modest stipend, to provide a foster home for the two boys and for the "minder" in exchange for her unpaid labour. Ewan accepted the money with relief and welcomed the sixteen-year-old Mhairi Livingstone when she arrived, but he greeted his young charges with resentful suspicion.

Life on Seil was not happy for the orphans. Neglected and maltreated by Ewan MacLean, with any signs of affection from Mhairi so vigorously discouraged by MacLean that she learnt to offer her support only rarely and in secret. Growing up under this loveless parent, for Hector and Mungo, harsh words, cruel blows and forced labour were their daily fare. Their only experience of love was a growing attachment to each other: their only comfort, the warmth of each other's bodies on the hard and narrow bed they were forced to share.

As they grew, MacLean demanded ever more from them around the farm, but gave them more blows than praise or leisure in return, but still, the boys found time to improve their poaching skills in Ballachuan Wood and learn to outwit the Laird's keepers.

Hector, always the bigger and stronger, really preferred to skip school and help on the farm, so his studies suffered badly, and his English remained slow and laboured. Mungo, in contrast, was a quick, enthusiastic scholar in both English and the Gaelic. This didn't always go well with their classmates. Mungo simply ignored being teased for being small, aloof, and a teacher's pet, but when Hector was taunted as big and slow, Mungo would react with violent rage, attacking the culprits, regardless of their age or strength.

In time, Ewan took Mhairi to be his partner, and she produced his child: a daughter of such sunny disposition that the whole household softened in her rays. Hector, the gentle giant, was especially enthralled, and grew very fond of the tiny new arrival.

Finally, the day came for the two young men to fulfil the bargain that had brought them to Seil. They must voyage to India and join the Army. Hector, at sixteen, was already old enough, and Mungo, fourteen, would qualify by the time the voyage was over. Places awaited them in India with the 74th Regiment of foot: the final, dangerous legacy from their dead benefactor. Hector, strong, and charming as he was, confident and self-possessed as he appeared to be, depended much upon his young companion, but for Mungo everything came second to his love for Hector. Each of them knew they had survived their childhood only because they had been together. They believed that only together, they would survive in India.

Our brave orphans were completely dazed by the boiling march from the Madras Dock, through the amazing sights, smells and sounds of their new world. A storm of loud, shouted, unfamiliar orders on arrival at Fort St George, was prelude to a confusing and anxious first encounter with India and the army. Mungo quickly grasped the unfamiliar orders, regulations and traditions, rephrasing them for Hector, with a word or two of Gaelic added here and there. Bit by bit, the two young islanders learned to cope with the life and routine of the Regiment, the climate, and the unfamiliar diet.

While striving to acclimatise, they had to also learn the complicated hierarchies of rank, race, and religion; and in these matters Mungo excelled; quite soon recognising who belonged to which culture, and even acquiring some grasp of the native tongues. He quickly established who was truly important to the common soldier, and who was merely the holder of high office. He became a great favourite with the sepoys, or native troops, and slowly earned the puzzled respect of his fellow countrymen. Hector proved to be a model soldier and gained the friendship and admiration of his comrades. He obeyed orders, looked smart and kept his cheerful smile whatever happened.

The 74th would now be deployed with forces of various Indian rulers, alongside troops of the British East India Company, popularly known as "John's Army". Among their main objectives was the defeat of Tipu Sultan, ruler of Mysore. Tipu's father, a Muslim general, had displaced his employer, the Hindu King of Mysore, and pursued the British forces to the very gates of Madras. Tipu had continued the family tradition with several victorious campaigns, and almost worst of all, now appeared to be making alliance with the French. With this objective, Hector and Mungo were marched across India, learning, maturing, and skirmishing for nearly four years. Ultimately, the target would be the island town and ancient fort of Seringapatam, the fabulous capital of Tipu Sultan's illegitimate but glittering rule over the State of Mysore.

Their full adventures need not be recorded here but, on the third of May 1799, the 74th Regiment of foot, commanded by Major General Baird, stormed the ramparts of Seringapatam. This was the fourth war with Tipu Sultan's family and there were scores to settle. The participants, Indian and British, were driven by bitter memories of earlier engagements. Thus, our two young men, in the company of eighty thousand fellow human beings, were thrust into one of the bloodiest and most celebrated episodes of Imperial history.

That first, dramatic assault was aided by a senior officer of the enemy serving inside the fort. He had secretly turned his allegiance away from Tipu Sultan and directed the defending troops away from the main point of assault. There followed some twenty-four hours of confusion and bloody carnage before Tipu Sultan was killed and Seringapatam was taken.

Amid the receding smoke, dust and looting, a group from the 74th, with an officer in charge, came upon the badly wounded and unconscious figure of Hector Campbell. His bloody head was cradled in the arms of his comrade, Mungo, also sorely wounded. Around them lay a ring of mutilated enemy dead.

That officer later reported that Private Mungo Grant, wounded and separated from his companions, had arrived at the scene only after Private Hector Campbell had slain or driven off the entire enemy party. This was confirmed by Grant, but not by Campbell himself, whose memory of events was obliterated by the severity of his wounds. It was officially recorded that, while details of the incident were confused, the affair had been significant to the victorious outcome of the day. Mungo's evidence, as reported above, was accepted by The Army, and Hector, recovering from his wounds, was hailed as a regimental hero. He was promoted to the rank of Sergeant forthwith and promised a sum of prize money unprecedented for a private soldier.

Hector and Mungo, much assisted by Hector's heroic standing, received honourable discharge from the Army as wounded, and the promised prize money made possible a very different return to Seil from that of their journey out, six years before. But, even with the Army's official goodwill behind them, it was a full year before they had

recovered from their wounds and boarded a suitable civilian ship.

The homeward voyage was a weary seven months and on arrival, they made an extended visit to Edinburgh, to enjoy fruits of their new prosperity amid the pleasures of that thriving capital. For the first time ever, they could live almost as gentry, and even obtained introductions to the Breadalbane lawyers, to arrange a fitting home to await them on return to Seil.

Hector and Mungo travelled on horseback, accompanied by a servant whose presence confirmed their new-found status as he tactfully guided them in social skills. The fine stone bridge to Seil, newly built when they had left, they now crossed as well-found tenants. Their new lease covered all the lands of Ballachuan Township , including the little patch where, as children, they had suffered under the now deceased Ewan MacLean.

Our heroes built a good solid house and began a hard-working life, very happy but making little outside contact beyond the demands of business and civility. The house was governed by Mhairi MacLean, once Livingstone, the minder of their infancy, supported by her daughter, Anne: no longer a little girl, but a very pretty teenager. These beloved and familiar ladies ruled a team of female servants indoors, while various outdoor workers attended to the farm and to the horses.

Perhaps because Ewen MacLean had ever spoken ill of his foster sons, some people remained suspicious of these prosperous heroes. Happily, the Minister of Kilbrandon Church was both friendly and supportive, though always mindful that some of his parishioners would rather hear him threaten hellfire than give praise for valour. He visited periodically, especially enjoying conversations with Mungo, for whom he had a growing respect.

For three or four years our veterans lived undisturbed, and Hector became a good farmer, remembering all that he had learned as a boy. It was a good time to be farming on Seil. The expanding slate quarries were attracting an ever-growing population of workers and families to consume the home-grown milk, oats, potatoes and meat.

Not unexpectedly, Hector eventually declared his feelings for Ann, the little girl he'd loved even before leaving for India. She accepted, of course, but insisted that any engagement should be extremely short and that she and Hector must have a house of their own. Mungo, always planner and director of their little kingdom, supervised the construction of a modest new dwelling, just a few yards from the existing house. This to be a home for himself and for Mhairi, who would transfer her governance to that new dwelling, leaving the old one to be, as Mungo phrased it, "The principal residence under the governance of Mistress Campbell, for occupation by herself and the Sergeant, who will continue as our Chief".

This arrangement was approved by all, and Mungo, though always strangely quiet and private, found peace to pursue his study and his reading, calling often at the manse, on the pretext of borrowing or returning books. Thus the orphaned heroes settled down and, for five or six years, lived a life of peace and comforting routine: it was not an enduring peace.

One afternoon Mungo'd friend, the Minister, while pottering in the garden by the Manse door, received an unexpected visitor.

"Good day, Minister: Major Leslie, of the 74th." Was his greeting, "I believe you might direct me to the gallant Sergeant Campbell, formerly of my regiment."

The minister smiled broadly. "Good day to you, Major. I can instantly provide you with an expert guide to Hector Campbell's place. Look behind you; his comrade, Mungo Grant, is approaching this very minute. The visitor turning to see Mungo, laughed aloud.

"Indeed, Minister, he will be the best guide in the world: he IS Hector Campbell".

Mungo simply dropped his eyes, but the Minister's reaction was surprise.

"My dear Sir, I assure you this is not Campbell but Grant". Come, Mungo, kindly put Major Leslie to rights".

"I think, Minister, we must first ask Major Leslie to explain himself." was as far as Mungo would reply.

"That's very easy, Sergeant", said the officer "I was present, a junior officer, at Seringapatam, and witnessed your outstanding valour. Being with my men, high up on the rampart far above you, we could be no help but had a perfect view of your victorious engagement. I can never forget the sight of your (forgive me) slight and youthful figure engaging and defeating the stream of native soldiers that issued from the little

The remains of the settlement of Druim, at the north of Ballachuan.

gate. Upon my soul, Sir; how could I be wrong? There could not have been another figure so young and so small, amongst all our troops. I would know you anywhere, although I learnt your name much later and only by hearsay".

Mungo stood silent for a moment. "Minister" he said, "may we discuss this further in the quietness of your room?" Once inside, Mungo embarked on his tale.

"In the fighting at Seringapatam, Separated from Hector and the others of our troop, I came suddenly upon a knot of Tipu Sultan's guards on duty at a small internal gate. Close by, lay a bloody, red-coated corpse that I took to be my Hector. Losing all control, I butchered those poor fellow-creatures in a wicked grief and rage. I continued in that bloodlust as other defenders issued from the gate. Only when they were no more, did I feel the pain of my wounds, and the full horror of my brutality. I then spotted Hector, further up the passage, fighting off an enemy soldier. At a shout from me, his assailant fled and Hector, sorely wounded, staggered down the passage to collapse into my arms. Soaking in his life's blood: I believed that Hector had given his life for me.

My wicked rage deserved no honour. Any reward must go only to Hector. So, for the Reporting Officer, I slightly tailored my report of the affair and ascribed the credit to him".

Finished his tale, Mungo stood up and walked to the window. The other two men were silent for a moment. Major Leslie was the first to speak.

"Mr Grant, I must assume that you would have this story go no further. I have long known of your courage, though only now I learn your name. I will guard the details of your secret and feel sure the Minister will do the same. But I shall make it my duty, far beyond the regiment, to make the names of Grant and Campbell properly renowned. It's an honour to meet you". He turned away and the minister, tears running down his face, stepped to the window and took Mungo by the hand. He could find no words, but his meaning was clear.

Major and Minister kept their promise. The names of Campbell and Grant are familiar to all who thoroughly understand that curious affair amid the heat of battle at Seringapatam.

Sergeant Campbell and his lady became highly respected by all around: producing a fine brood of children, whose descendants are to be found in the County to this day.

More relaxed and content, now that his secret had been shared, Mungo met chiefly with the more bookish of his neighbours but was consulted by many others, for wise advice counsel. His principal pleasure in life was to observe the development and welfare of the growing family next door. He lived into respectable old age, faithfully attended by Mhairi, and always ready to share a quiet dram with Hector, his beloved comrade and foster brother.

Volunteer Gunners of Seil and Easdale.

SEIL ISLAND: ARMY AND EMPIRE

The island town and now-ruined fort of Srirangapatna lies 15 miles from Mysore town, capital of the former princely State of Mysore. The British called it Seringapatam. It was an ancient stronghold of the Hindu Maharajas, until they were ousted by Hyder Ali in 1761. Hyder declared himself Sultan of Mysore, and the title passed to his son Tipu Sultan. Tipu was a ruthless soldier who had considerable success against British expansion in India. He was also a very talented and cultured collector and commissioner of art.

The death of Tipu and fall of Seringapatam were crucial to the British interest, and their re-instatement of the original Hindu ruling family was an important precedent for future relations with local rulers in all the Princely States of India.

There are historic excuses for making the connection between Seil and 18th century India. In the Kilbrandon House of my childhood, there was a series of large prints depicting the fall of Seringapatam. The final print, "Surender of Tipu Sultan's Sons", included a group of British officers standing around as the unfortunate young men were led out from a fanciful artistic impression of Seringapatam. An archivist and historian who visited the house knew the pictures, and identified several of these men by name as the offspring of Argyllshire lairds.

Many such lairds, finding rents raised from their land inadequate for a gentleman's lifestyle, had two principal ways of raising money: a good marriage or military service under the Crown. An officer's pay in the Army or Navy was not a fortune, but prize money, which was essentially a share in the loot of conquest, could be sufficient to build a new house and cover expenses for a couple of generations.

A military tradition had long existed in the Highlands, be it fighting rival clans or the armed raiding of cattle. After the 1745 uprising, the government recruited Highlanders to keep them out of mischief and to supplement the armies of Empire. An army career for the orphan boys of our tale is therefore not unlikely. That military tradition continued right into the 20th century, when the Volunteer Gunners, raised from the quarrymen of Seil and Easdale Islands, served in the South African War.

POSTSCRIPT

Perhaps the foregoing stories and articles may suggest that Seil Island's centuries of traumatic events leave a local history with little logic and no discernible theme or progress.

They speak of frequent change, sometimes annihilating one settled community after another, sometimes so slow and stealthy that only the more observant understood their significance. In all events, it appears that human nature is a constant: the same conflicts of folly and weakness versus wisdom and fortitude were to be found in the earliest settlers, as they are to be found in us today.

Another constant is the ever-blessed beauty of Seil's natural surroundings. Unchanged are the wave-battered shores to the west and the sheltered waters on the eastern coast, the calm havens, and the peaceful, inland crofts. Many views have been unchanged in centuries. In some, ancient structures are decaying: vanishing reminders of departed people and events. These enduring scenes are captured for us in the photographs by Trevor Davies.

Seil is the product of each generation dealing with change in its own way, in its own times. Repeatedly, the map has been redrawn as populations waxed and waned. Everything was new and strange in its time; be it the first stone building or the first village. We may regret the retreat of farming, the fading of ceilidhs and of Gaelic speech; but greater changes have come before, and the island magic has always prevailed.

Some worry because, in the past thirty years, a lot of new houses were built, but the population fell with fewer children and young people. Almost all growth has been along the road, creating in places, something almost semi-urban. It's largely attractive, comfortable, and well-built, but very different from anything seen here in the past.

No Agency or Government will show serious or practical interest. As always, Seil must depend on those who live here and love their island. All these islands can only be the offspring of their history. Fortunately, history suggests we can be optimistic. Our errors are usually obscured by the benign providence of Nature.

Looking west from above Seaview across Ellenabeich and Easdale Island to the south-east coast of the island of Mull.

The Sun setting behind An Grianan, seen from Puilladobhrain.